Viewed From the Keel of a Canoe

by
J. Matthew Boyleston

∞

EDUCE PRESS

Educe Press
Butte, MT

Published in the United States of America
First Edition, 2016

Library of Congress Catalogue-in-Publication
Data
J. Matthew Boyleston 2016--
        Viewed From the Keel of a Canoe
ISBN: 978-0-9965716-2-3

Cover Design by Igor Zelenov

educepress.com
facebook.com/educepress
twitter.com/educepress

For my grandfathers

Contents

Bird Killing

Since this is your grandmother's house too far in the county for cable;
since it's light till eight o'clock and you can see;
where the puzzles miss pieces and your father's box of leftover stuff
    in his bedroom has nothing new,
    where the yearbooks are signed "with love"
by women who are not your mother;
after supper and dishes, past the dog pen, the hogs,
past the line of pecans that point to the buried corners of a burned-out house,
after walking as far as you can go and come back before dark,
    where the combine rusts;
    where you grasp for a sling shot from your back pocket,
and you've scoured a stone from the ground,
gone quiet to pick a sound from the night,
since you've found your direction and your relative place,
                                        you begin with a wren.

Gas Station

Burned out brick, slunk and gutted in the brush,
my grandfather's gas station is forgotten.

I never got the full story, not from him,
but growing up, when we drove by

the glassed-out windows and gray, bare pumps,
the kudzu thickly steeping in the heat,

I felt an awkward sort of pride, like finding a gravestone
in the woods that bares your name. I felt that this was mine.

He taught me once to pump gas, (I'd forgotten this)
trusting the clumsy handle in a kid's hands,

telling me how so I could understand—but slowly,
as the station veined with vines and graffiti,

our language grew apart.
I lost the lilt and swagger of my voice.

When we moved to the suburbs where every eyesore
is demolished, all embarrassments tucked away,

he moved on to other rundown jobs:
farmer, foreman, picker on the local radio.

I didn't visit—his voice an eyesore overgrown
with accents I couldn't understand.

It costs more to tear it down,
than let it rot.

Pig Needle

Air is the dead smell of pigs.

I break through rust.
I spread mice like buckshot
and kick husks up in clouds.

Nothing suckles, nothing trotters
in a room that is black water come alive,
where the diamondback and dust moth
slide on dry skin and with dry wings.

Past barbed wire and cow pasture,
into a corner of my grandfather's farm,
I've come into the farrowing house
for the first time to see for myself
a sound I once heard hid behind its tin door.

The incubating bulb had splotched the hall
like a monarch's wing. The men went in and shut me out
and then I heard it, almost like a person, scream.

The room thickens like slop in a trough
so I cannot see. Hands on the floor,
I finger a dried birthmark or the stain
left from cutting hogs from boars.

But from an open drawer, light rises—
a needle rusting in its used syringe,
its eye scabbed with iron, a serum
for the babies so they grow strong and big,
the ones like us that hear before they see.

The room warms me like the stomach of a pig.

Coppermouth

We trace divergence.

We are in an old van
on an old bridge
looking for signs:

a snake slip,
a warm nest,
the traces of thought
when we all were one.

The earth has Alzheimer's.
It forgets all it ever knew—
bits and pieces of a shattered memory
flashing up at us
when we dig deep.

The evolutionary herpetologist
from the county zoo
with thick waders
and a rusted S-hook
is down on his hands and knees
peering into a dark swamp

and we students fan out in all directions
searching for the Coppermouth,
extinct ancestor
of moccasin and pit-viper,
a slithering rumor
someone somewhere had heard tell.

Our Gullah translator,
comes back with filtered stories
and the feral bodies
of two boa constrictors
let loose in the swamp.

But beneath the stories,
there is something here:
wounds that don't respond to anti-venom
like a door that won't open
with a key that fits,
the occasional sloughed skin
with patterns both foreign and familiar
to ones we know,
even, perhaps, two rotten fangs
tacked to the rafter of a hunter's lodge.

If such a species were still alive,
we must find it. If only to show
us the process of our combination
and how different we've become.

If only to remind us of the God
who looks down on us saying:
come together all things
in my name.

At the Salkehatchie

Slowly, I evolve into a world of pure bird—
the purple bunting,

brant and barn owl,
the bobwhite quail,

the roll of the wood duck's head,
the hummingbird's pursed lips.

Landscape with sand spur—
hydrangea, gardenia,

wren and jessamine.

~

In the lung-dark water,
the soft shell of the freshwater turtle.

North Fork and South Fork,
Cattawba, Savannah, Saluda, Edisto—

a river black with red tannin,
the world's longest black river.

Swamp Fox and Gamecock.
God in the thunder,

in the incoming storm.

~

Here, in the swallowing stillness,
the world is only as new
as the mind of the nearest infant.
Life diminished, life regained.

Every hidden sin is a doe suckling young.
In the Garden of Eden,
Adam cleans his gun.
Though we cling to the graveyard in the garden,

Come.

Viewed From the Keel of a Canoe

Morning—   a crane cocked on the dock's lip.

From the keel of the canoe,
       I rotate on the face of the lake.

A man is a tissue structure
       to hold back the flood—
Adam, a dam,
              flues open, hydroelectric,
       the Saluda River
coursing cold beneath the water's weight
       —like teeth, the concrete underbite of the world.

       When you reach your hand
into the green darkness—the lake descends,
resisting you, the human touch—meniscus—

your hand gloved in hydrangea that chokes the lake.

In the winter, waters recede—bleached beach toys
and cement blocks burying gravestones,
where the power company had sealed an abandoned town—
        rotten coffins floating on the surface of the water

—garfish, rock bass, channel cats, a school of brim—

what we've created,
        towns sunken,
a landscape swollen with a misplaced river,
the bottomland and the timberland beneath the canoe and the full moon.

I first caught a fish in the dock's shoals,
        found a rock seat, quartz, in the shore's erosion.

Paddling away from the Jetski's pollution,
noise confined to the cove's circle,

        where sound carries—the bird wing, and lightning freezing on the water's glass,

life seen from inside the atom,
where blue becomes silver becomes white becomes blue.

Ordered Fragments

Hard cake of the clay shore,
the lake leeched back,
trees tinseled with snakes.

From the vantage of our dock,
a moccasin beds a dead fish
in the cotton of its mouth.

~

In the pull of the foxhounds,
my grandfather bounds
through the cracked air and parched scrub.

A red splotch of bald fur,
a pile of dead foxes
pelted tight to the ground.

~

Split from the tongue of God —
the Muskogean name for the gurgle of water
my ancestor willed to the Lord.

I affirm total immersion.
I drink sweet, sweet tea steeped
in the deep water of a healing spring.

~

In Adam's broken nucleus the neutrons run free—
the tangram of memory,
the bell-shaped chapel of the womb,

chronos and kairos,
an armor of light,

a single incandescent bulb slung from the worn rafter.

~

The salamander's atomic orange,
the smolder of my tongue's flame—

from my body, the burst of wings.

What Prayer Will Not Do

It will not paint a still lake in your mind,
perhaps at sundown, with happy little trees
and a lone boat rusting in the weeds of the shore.

It will not come with a child proof cap
in an orange bottle—take twice a day
for anxiety or inflammation—
call me in the morning.

Give what is desired:
a quick glimpse of a girl,
a new car, big muscles,
a perfect score,
or peace deep in the heart,
that great myth,
the golden fleece.

No pathways in space will be opened.
No symphonies written,
no hair re-grown,
no addictions kicked,
no remission.

Every morning, every evening
in a closed up room as Christ commands,
I light a failing candle,
genuflect, and whisper so my wife won't hear:

Pater noster, Ave Maria,
Our Father, Hail Mary,
full of grace—speak softly
till the throat goes raw

and discipline, like I train my toddler niece,
my mind—don't go there,
don't touch that—and turn away,

then no and again no and no.

Besides, who really says:
I'm down with the
Deus absconditus,
the absent God.

We sing:
I have climbed the highest mountains,
I have run through the fields
only to be with you.

But prayer is the ultimate
unfunded mandate
and 401-K.

We say:
I don't pray to change God.
I pray to change myself.

Exactly, but into what?

And then it comes:
the deepest embarrassment—
Have we met before?
I've forgotten your name?

Dear God
My Lord
Hey You?

but this—
what prayer will not do—

heal you.

In Back of the Hog Parlor

the small pond of pig scum hosed from cement pens
slowly swallowed my grandfather's prize heifer.

I was ten and waded out with him into the slop
bearing a brace of 2x4s to wedge beneath her belly

and lift her from the sucking mud.
She brayed like to wake the dead, fecklessly,

with instinctual fear no one could have bred out of her,
flailing the filth like a terrified child caught in the winter covers

We worked on her until our light was gone—useless—all of it.
My grandfather said shit and shot her twice in the head.

In My Father's House

In the beginning,
God created the world
to the Adagio of Mozart's Clarinet Concerto in A Major.

All opens before me—
an isosceles sky,
rent cotton,
the white steeple of a Baptist church:
this is the setting for all stories.

But how to make you understand?
To be understood?—
a janitor fingering for a flipped breaker
in the basement of a school.

Books become latitudes
and latitudes books

like remembering the town
you grew up in, the house
in which Miss Havisham lived.

I will now list the blessings I've received:
a swift kick in the ass,
synthesis, association, allergies
a cup half empty and half full,
$a^2 + b^2 = c^2$,
the lines of earth.

But here is the thing about the prodigal son—
who didn't raise him right to begin with?

My father once set the church roof on fire
with Roman candles on the Fourth of July.

Dead pumpkins
melting behind the shed all year.
My grandfather surprisingly heavy in his casket
like a ripe melon dug from the vine.

Life was grass stains and the sap from trees.
There were open fields,
then a sign in an open field *For Sale*,
then a field with a nursing home in it,
then a nursing home with the memory of a cotton field.

Life in the wasteland of the chestnut blight.

Knowing enthusiasm means "God in us."

Knowing nothing but the Sandhills and the Edisto.

Memory, imagination:
no one comes to the father but through me.

For the Means of Grace and for the Hope of Glory

With the tuft of his hind hoof,
the wild colt lunges
for the long felt of his wet nose—

an impossible maneuver,
one act of feckless grace,
the taste of mulchy horse on my tongue.

It is not as though God's Word has failed

There is a rainbow over Houston.
The devil beats his wife.
A clogged highway,
and a man,
and a motorcycle,
and a sign on an overpass blinking on-and-off:
drink, drive, go to jail.

I know all the words to *Gimme Shelter*.

In third grade,
I spread rumors about a kid
in my class with a deformed face
who lived with two women
near my house. He wore the same
grey sweatpants every day to school.
Every day he came to our front door
to ask if I could come out to play
baseball or walk in the woods.
I told everyone that he had AIDS.

I called myself a Gentile until I was ten.

Let's say nothing about the ATM
in the narthex of a mega-church downtown,
nothing of the swipes and keypads
on the offering plates.
Let's say I hear the King James Bible
in the voice of my first preacher,
Pastor Corder who died when I was seven.
I can't remember a thing about his face
but I hear his voice every day, every hour.

There is a cold-case file on the death of God.

On the morning after Halloween,

I walk with my dad in a pine wood
built on the dead body of a cotton field,
row on row of neatly seeded
young white pine. We walk
a mile or more to get out
of the man-made woods
and step into a clearing,
where the kudzu grows square
around the floorboards of a rotten house.
In the lacing sun,
appliance doors, grey fenders,
bright white sinks strewn out
like gravestones in the light.
An icebox from the twenties
stands upright, door closed.
Astonished, we open it:
inside a glass milk bottle,
unbroken, undisturbed.
I break the cap and pour out clean,
pure milk that has not soured.

I've got you where I want you is in his voice.

Run off the road, disoriented
with a broken kick drum in my chest,
a song I know comes on the radio
and I begin to sing,
full throated,
at the top of my lungs
with the voice God gave me:

It is not as though God's word has failed.
I know all the words to *Gimme Shelter*.
I called myself a Gentile until I was ten.
There is a cold-case file on the death of God.
I've got you where I want you is in his voice.
Love me like I should be loved.

19

Gray Fox

For years, my grandfather shared
his garden with a rare gray fox.

As he piddled about, the fox
watched from the wood's edge,

in enfleshed silence,
following every slow movement

my grandfather made.
Once he died, we neglected

his garden, a filigree
of dried vines on rusted cages.

The fox puttered about his own
sweet business in those eroded rows.

Last night, while walking
I was suddenly startled

by a soft sound in the grass—
here, in the fold of the garden,

a mother fox and her skulk
of young kit bed down.

Self-Portrait from Ordered Fragments

There is the desert
        that is a slow wick,
        and the cactus and the highway
        defiled in waves of heat.
There is the desert of this blank page
        where waters freeze
        and are released at the first light.
Water and salt water.
        When Hugo hit these shores
        people fled. Houses were torn
        like families, trees uprooted
        like sons. Storms clashed dunes,
        bagged, re-bagged. The aired salt
        coated a new coast in its icing.
There is the blood moon
        striped to peppermint by clouds.
There is the sliver of a gravestone on my shelf
        split by kudzu from an antebellum
        cemetery in Orangeburg,
        and it spells MARGARET.
There is the field beyond the vineyard, beyond the orchard,
        where a shuttered, clapboard farmhouse burned
        leaving four brick sentinels
        no one will curl up to in winter.
There is Miguel Marti i Pol
        with Multiple Sclerosis,
        he writes in Catalan.
        He hears the breath's rhythm
        "When someone makes love with a nubile girl."
There are the antiques of my grandmother's house,
        where every scratch of teak wood,
        every broken doll
        the groove-worn records of the victrola,
        recall the lingering wings of the dead.
There is the deck of cards,
        in four suits, aristocratic,

who will continually lose
their crispness in the shuffle of our hands.
There are vowels.
There is the blue heron on my dock,
a curved question mark.
There are many birds on the branch at my kitchen window.
The creak of hardwood floors
breathing back and forth at night when the frost sets
There is the bookshelf my grandfather built as a boy
to hold his Latin grammar
that still smells of the tobacco barn
where he plied the wood.
There is the guitar,
that was left behind by my uncle,
a long crack beneath the pick guard.
All is multiplication and division,
Sines, Cosines, and Tangents,
numbers I can no longer add
without counting my fingers.
There is a porcelain doorknob,
a paperweight from a dead house on my desk.
There is Michael,
my cousin, who lives alone
working glass to stained-glass,
he goes to sea two times a year,
a ship's engineer, and we will not hear
from him for months on end.
There is the artery tug of an Otis Redding song,
and my father who pleads with the Lord
"to please let Otis have whatever it is he wants."
There is both Epithalamion and Prothalamion.
What is released
when the gas pipe opens?
when the glacier moves?
when the Galapagos Tortoise
breathes his last breath,
the one whose shell was dated by Darwin?
What is released when wood warps,

when guitars buckle under the pressure of six strings?
All is kinetic and potential energy,
      I have memorized geology,
      I still forget the ground below your feet.
What is released when we wake
      in the morning to the slant light
      through Venetian blinds
      written across our eyes?
What is in the hollow arc of my mouth?
There is enormity.
There is vast openness.
There is the voice of a blank continent
      calling for jungle.
And what there is not
      is a dark storm
      slowly forming on the Gulf of Mexico.

Prayer is a Disease of the Will

I felt it first
in my left breast,
a hard lump
like dried sugar
clumped in the bowl.

As it slowly spread,
I said "dear Lord"
and "My God"
lowering myself
with care to my aching knees
and clasping the skin
to fling it out.

I couldn't do a thing
I wanted: teach school,
play golf, drink beer—
the fevers,
the night-sweats
a fine yellow brine
on my skin,
my changing smell.

It migrated
to my lower jaw
and my lumped tongue
flopped in my mouth
like a dying fish.

Spraying "Gawth,
Gawth," I screamed
with dry breath
and fog and fresh decay.

I could not follow
my lack of speech

with words.

When it entered
my lymph nodes,
a long siege.

I laid down all arms
and reveled in the warm
burn through my limbs
like an IV drip,
imagining morphine,
sounding out *metastasize*
no pain, no feeling.

Suddenly, the hospice nurse—
deadly syrettes
like fresh cigarettes
on my bedside table.

But still, I could not
go through with any action.

Christ should have come
as an EMT
because the body
demands repair, to be refinished,
is worth more
than a Louis XIV
or a Shaker hutch—

But all I wanted,
what I was wanting
was to gum:
Kyrie Eleison
Kyrie Eleison—

Lord have mercy,
have mercy on us.

If it were not so I would have told you

Memory moves through monastic silence:

I go room by room—
depression glass, lazy Susan,
paper Santa in a domed display.

But still there is no sound or smell:
no aloe vera or touch of whiskey in the wood,
not even the singular descending cheer
of purple martins from the martin house—

or deeper still—
a well-tempered clavier,
the carol of the bells,
the tintinnabulation of our DNA.

I practice patience
and see what in the stillness I can recall—

a square field,
a rhombus of cotton,
the world as Euclid viewed it,

sandhills, red clay and loam,
the body of memory, its back stretched long
across the bottomland,
the bloated carcass of thought
floating up from a black river,

or even a disembodied secret—
mouthing out *Tintagel*
early on Easter morning alone in my room.

There is a new shadow on a windowpane,
a wren attempting to come inside,
haint in the body of a small brown bird,

the woman who passed away in this very room,

but I know better, the bird is a moving memory
in continual change,

the driveway was gravel
and then it was not,
the sycamore tree in the church alley sloughed bark
and then it didn't,

the shed without power was black with dust and clutter,
like the circular web of a brown recluse,
and then it was opened,

or, to take a different view,
I read *Journey to the Center of the Earth*,
reclined in the music room
of a house I no longer know,

but the wren that knocks the glass is not a wren,
she is a sparrow
and lights on a limb beyond
my kitchen window,
she lights on the lip of a puddle of mud,
in the bosom of the earth
now turned to its own purpose.

In the Bell Yard
Trinity Cathedral, Columbia SC

Below the low hang of live oak and palmetto,
among gravestones grown green with envy of the living,
among the three Wade Hamptons wound in wrought iron,
I sit in the shade of Henry Timrod and listen
to the slow, long ringing of the bells.

These words will rub off our minds
like epitaphs exposed to salt and wind.
An ode, a state hymn, all of his I know,
ride on a tide of melody and ceremony.

Before the evensong, in a slanting sun,
what in time is more than words or names?
What will last beyond the grave and gravestone,
survive divorce, names split like granite,
survive our need to sign ourselves in stone?
What things in this world are blessed
without the sweat of permanence?

What is left of the Christian?
The decay of a fertile grave,
a cathedral filled with air,
the transubstantiation which is passed,
the consubstantiation which cannot feed us,

or the echo of a day at the Battery in 1867
in the mind of an old man who's father's father was there
at the dedication to the Confederate dead,
who took in the same salt-and-sweat air that Timrod breathed?

At what point do we begin to say without saying:
enough—this house to house religion is a museum,

a reliquary of a faith drowned in the swamps of nouns and verbs
inarticulate, confined, ephemeral, ignoble?

Even the Hamptons have turned to stone
and Henry Timrod, Confederate, Episcopal, is voiceless.

What options have we left ourselves?
Who would score a mass for the end of time?

And in the echo in the bell yard,
fingers running the rivulets of the gravestones—

Of ourselves we make cathedrals.
Not from our words
as Wordsworth wanted;
but from here,
where my hands that hold
you are two chapels
and the green glaze of my eyes
is slow stained glass,
where my arms around you
are a flying buttress
and the cross of my body
on your body
is the long central hall
of a cruciform church
rising higher and higher
to my chest's clerestory;
the pattern of aisles,
each ripple of skin,
a row of pews;
your rolling, parted wave
of wood-burnished hair
a choir—and in the great
bell tower my mouth
resounds with the ring
of a kiss calling forth
the pregnant tension
among three people,
before the beginning

of the word,
this tension which will
suffice—

the unspoken sound
of two restless tongues
in primal eloquence

awaiting the arrival of a child.

About the Author

J. Matthew Boyleston is the Associate Provost for Academic Technology and former Dean of the School of Fine Arts at Houston Baptist University. He holds a PhD in creative writing and literature from the University of Houston and a received an M.F.A. from the University of South Carolina. He has taught at Bloomsburg University in Pennsylvania and at the Malahide Language School in Dublin, Ireland. His poems and essays have appeared widely in such journals as *Confrontation*, the *Spoon River Poetry Review*, *Blackwell's Companion to Creative Writing* and *Puerto del Sol*. He lives in Houston with his wife and two daughters.

Earlier versions of these poems were released in the following publications:

Confrontation: "Viewed from the Keel of a Canoe"
GSU Review: "Bird Killing"
The Imaginative Conservative: "For the Means of Grace and for the Hope of Glory", "Gray Fox", "Ordered Fragments", "Self-Portrait from Ordered Fragments"
Permafrost: "In Back of the Hog Parlor"
Powhatan Review: "In the Bell Yard"
Roanoke Review: "Gas Station"
Spoon River Poetry Review: "Pig Needle"
A Time of Singing: "Coppermouth"
Tipton Poetry Journal: "In My Father's House"
Transgressive Culture: "It is not as though God's Word has failed", "Prayer is a Disease of the Will", "What Prayer Will Not Do".

∞

THANK YOU

Made in the USA
Las Vegas, NV
20 December 2021